A VISIT TO THE

SESAME STREET

FIREHOUSE

A Random House PICTUREBACK®

A VISIT TO THE

by Dan Elliott • illustrated by Joe Mathieu

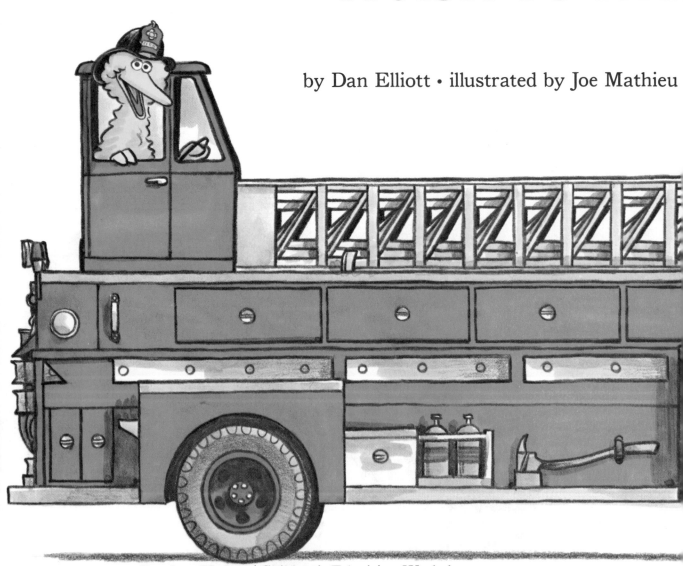

Random House / Children's Television Workshop

CTW
SESAME STREET FIREHOUSE

**Featuring Jim Henson's
Sesame Street Muppets**

Library of Congress Cataloging in Publication Data:
Elliott, Dan. A visit to the Sesame Street firehouse. (A Pictureback book) SUMMARY: The fire chief shows the Sesame Street characters how fire fighters fight fires and the equipment at the firehouse. 1. Fire stations—Juvenile literature. 2. Fire extinction—Juvenile literature. [1. Fire departments. 2. Fire extinction. 3. Puppets] I. Henson, Jim. II. Mathieu, Joseph, ill. III. Sesame Street (Television program) IV. Children's Television Workshop. V. Title. TH9148.E44 1983 628.9'25 83-4606 ISBN: 0-394-86029-2 (pbk.); 0-394-96029-7 (lib. bdg.)
Manufactured in the United States of America

One day Big Bird, Ernie, and Grover came running into Mr. Hooper's store all out of breath.

"Mr. Hooper! There's a fire across the street!" said Big Bird.

Mr. Hooper looked out the window. Little wisps of smoke were coming from the window on the third floor of the empty building across the street. "Stay right here," said Mr. Hooper. "I will call the fire department."

When Mr. Hooper's call came, the fire fighter at the desk sounded the alarm. All the fire fighters in the firehouse stopped what they were doing. Some were polishing the trucks. Some were making a snack. Some were taking naps. The alarm woke them up.

They slid down the fire pole and quickly put on their fire-fighting clothes. They were ready. And so was Hydra, the fire dog!

One of the fire fighters ran outside to stop the traffic. "Okay! All clear!" he called.

The sirens blared and the fire trucks roared out of the firehouse.

In a few minutes the pumper truck, followed by the hook-and-ladder truck, came tearing down Sesame Street.

The driver of the pumper truck connected a large hose to the fire hydrant while three fire fighters ran into the building to see how far the fire had spread. In seconds they were back.

"There's too much smoke to go upstairs! Get the ladder!"

The fire fighters on the hook-and-ladder truck put the ladder up to the third-floor window, where the smoke was now pouring out.

A fire fighter quickly put on a special mask and air tank to protect himself from smoke and climbed up the ladder. Smash! He broke the window and pointed the hose inside. Water sprayed into the smoky room.

Slowly the smoke began to clear. Other fire fighters went into the building with more hoses. At last the fire was out.

When Mr. Hooper said it was safe, Big Bird, Ernie, and Grover went across the street to thank the fire fighters. Then Big Bird saw the fire fighter wearing his special mask.

"Help!" screamed Big Bird, and he ran to hide behind Grover.

"Don't be afraid," said the fire fighter. "This mask keeps me from breathing in too much smoke. And underneath every mask is a friendly fire fighter. See?" He took off the mask and smiled at Big Bird. Then he had an idea. "How would you and your friends like to visit the firehouse tomorrow?"

Everyone said yes all at once!

The next day Big Bird, Ernie, and Grover went to the firehouse.
The chief was ready to give them the grand tour.

"The firehouse is like a second home for us," said the chief as he took them upstairs. "We make our meals here and we eat here."

"This looks like a living room," said Ernie.

"It is," said the chief. "We can read a book, relax, or even take naps here. That's why we have cots. Sometimes fire fighters work all day and night without going home, and they need to take naps.

"But the most important thing we do when we're not fighting a fire is clean and test the equipment."

"Fire fighters wear special clothes, called turnout gear," said the chief. "Our rubber pants snap onto our boots so we can jump into both very quickly. Every fire fighter wears a helmet and rubber coat and gloves. Sometimes we have to wear a fireproof rescue suit to save people. If there is a lot of smoke, we carry an air tank and mask in case we need it to breathe."

"Oh, I saw one of those yesterday!" said Big Bird.

The chief let Ernie try on a turnout suit.

"I'm a space man!" said Ernie.

"That's right, Ernie," said the chief. "There is space for three of you in that suit!" Everybody laughed.

Then the chief showed them a big coil of hose. "Every fire truck carries a hose to put out fires. Sections of hose are screwed together to make one very long hose. Our truck has a hose that is more than five blocks long! When it is full of water, it is very heavy and will not bend."

"We use a fire axe to smash windows or chop down locked doors to save people trapped inside.

"Fire fighters need lots of special equipment to help them fight fires," said the chief. "Hooks or pike poles are used to pull down ceilings, poke holes in walls, and pry open windows so that heat and smoke can escape.

"We can get to a fire from the outside of a building by using a ladder. Some ladders can reach up to the thirteenth floor of a building! They shoot up from the truck like a jack-in-the-box."

"Is water the only way to put out a fire?" asked Ernie.

"No," said the chief. "Water won't stop gasoline from burning. So if a car or an airplane is on fire, we use foam. Foam is made by adding chemicals to water. A special 'foam gun' is attached to the roof of a pumper truck, and it shoots foam at the fire!"

"Often fog is the best way to put out a fire," the chief continued. "Just by turning the nozzle of a hose, a fire fighter can make a fine spray like fog or mist come out. It cuts through heat and smoke so fire fighters can get closer to where the fire is."

"This is our longest fire truck—the hook-and-ladder truck. It is so long that two people have to steer it—the driver in front and the tiller man in back. The tiller man steers the rear wheels to get the truck around corners."

Big Bird got behind the wheel in the back. "Hey, everybody, I'm a tiller bird!" he shouted.

Grover looked at the other trucks in the firehouse. "Why do you have so many trucks?" he asked.

"Each one has a special purpose," said the chief.

"Pumpers are hose trucks. They are the first trucks at a fire. The fire fighters on a pumper connect a short, thick hose between the fire hydrant and the hose on the pumper. The engine on the truck is used to pump water very fast and very hard.

"The rescue truck goes wherever there is a big fire. It is also sent on special calls to save people in trouble. It carries lots of special tools and equipment.

"The ambulance also goes wherever there is a big fire. It carries first-aid supplies for injured people. It can also take people to the hospital."

"My cousin Fred lives in the country and he doesn't have a fire hydrant near his house. What would happen if his house or barn was on fire?" asked Ernie.

"That's a good question," said the chief. "When there is a fire in the country, fire fighters use a special truck called a tanker-pumper. It carries its own water supply in a giant tank. Fire fighters can also use ponds, streams, lakes, and even swimming pools to provide water to wet down barns and homes."

"What if there's a fire on a boat?" asked Ernie.

"A fireboat is used to fight fires on ships and docks and in buildings along the waterfront. It fills its hose by pumping water right out of the river or bay."

Grover had a question too. "How do you fight forest fires?"
"We fight them on the ground with small fire trucks
called forestry trucks. Forestry trucks carry their
own water tank, pump, and hose.

"We also fight forest fires from the sky!"

"You mean fire fighters can *fly*?" said Big Bird.

The chief laughed. "No, but *planes* can. We fly very low in airplanes or helicopters and spray water and chemicals to put the fire out."

"Wow, you sure have to know a lot to be a fire fighter!" said Big Bird.

"And you must be so strong!" said Grover.

"Can I be a fire fighter when I grow up?" asked Ernie.

"If you can pass the test," the chief said. "In the meantime, there is a lot you can do to *prevent* fires.

"Every home should have a smoke detector. If a fire starts when you are asleep, an alarm will wake you up so you can get out safely and call the fire department.

"Don't play with matches—EVER! And don't play with the knobs on the kitchen stove.

"Don't play near electrical heaters.

"Ask your parents to write down your local fire emergency phone number and tape it to the wall near the phone."

"That's what Mr. Hooper did!" said Ernie.

Finally it was time to go home. Ernie, Grover, and Big Bird thanked the chief for letting them visit.

"I'll tell Bert all about the fire station," said Ernie.

"I'll tell Snuffy all about the hose. It looks a little like his snuffle," said Big Bird.

"I will tell my mommy all about EVERYTHING!" said Grover.

Then they shook hands with the chief. Hydra wanted to shake too. Everybody waved good-bye.